STRAY

a journey in, through, and out of faith

STRAY

a journey in, through, and out of faith

sarah jane pyper

STRAY
First Edition Trade Book, 2022
Copyright © 2022 by sarah jane pyper

To order additional books:
www.sarahjanepyper.com

Visit www.sarahjanepyper.com for more information

Published by Pyper Publishing

ISBN: 979-8-9871198-0-8

E-book also available

Editorial: Kerry Wade, kerriganwade.com
Book Design: Nskvsky
Printed in the USA by IngramSpark

To all those who allowed me to doubt
without ever doubting me

Contents

BEFORE

CHILD OF GOD

My image of God was only that
as told to me by my mother

An unconditional being residing in the gray
she told me

How else can he determine the spirit
if only with the individual on their independent path

God has a sense of humor
she told me

Through all our trials and tribulations
how else have we found the courage to laugh

God is a comfort
she didn't have to tell me

I saw it in her eyes
I heard it in her prayers

And I was thankful to have grown with a God
she told me
cares

sarah jane pyper

SACRAMENT

It was always a constant
welcoming as the warmth of the sun
on my skin
as sunrise is a relief
a strength to combat chaos
knowing light would pursue darkness always
and again
      and again
          and again

A SEED TO SOW

My faith began as a seedling
and as I was growing
roots were burrowing
engraving and encompassing
an embedded foundation
branches of community
nurtured and nourished
a glorious and magnificent tree
I could hold the weight
of the world on my shoulders
confident in the plan I so freely followed
it was a comfort to be told I was chosen
to believe I had someone up there rooting for me
a reason to look on the bright side
a reason to be patient
a reason to triumph over taunts and trials
I basked in the knowledge
there was a reason for everything
and held a firm grip to the bark
providing me protection and
offering me shade

MIDDLE CHILD

My persona spent its life in others' arms
who was I if not a vessel used to charm?
a crave for control with a passionate fire of a soul
a middle child grown old

THE GOLDEN CHILD

In my youth
I earned the Midas Touch—
burdened with the responsibility
to create worth
to define the value of the loved ones
I turned to gold
on hands and knees
burnished their wounds
polished their insecurities
I became the artist burnt
out from the statues I maintained
content to withdraw
in grease stains and sprained limbs
proof of the time I sacrificed
to value those I loved
above myself

HEART OF GOLD

Heaven help the child with a heart of gold
too heavy to carry on their own

PERFECTIONIST

I picked apart every piece of myself
until I was nothing of what I expected
if I could not fix it immediately
it would not be fixed at all
I fixed myself
to a pedestal
convinced myself I was tall
my fingers bleeding
clinging to the podium
to avoid the tragic fall

NOT ME HARDLY

Don't mistake the laughter for happiness
I was just terrified of what came in silence
life of the party
not me hardly
but I'd only show the parts of me they liked

STRAY

WEIGHT OF OTHERS

I was so busy holding their weight on my shoulders
I never thought it'd cause
me
to
sink

11

OVERTHINKER

My brain was so overrun by others' thoughts
I left no room for my own

ELEVEN

I was eleven
and I held my father's salvation in my arms
weekly reminders
I would never see him in heaven
I needed to be a missionary
I needed to be watchful of what
he tried to preach to me
I needed to pray for him to find himself
because he must not have wanted a family in eternity
but I still saw him every weekend
and listened while he explained his woe
so I played protector as a child to a father
who was in a battle against his own soul
and I went to church and wrestled with my thoughts
and tried to find comfort and peace
but I was a child who was told
my family was never going to be whole each week
and I spent my youth wondering why
my father didn't love me
and it's only because he happened to not believe
what I believed

I AM WHO RAISED ME

We were the only children of divorce
I heard the whispers in the ward
the proclamation to proclaim
my mother tried her best
but was it enough?
was she to blame for our independence
a household without the priesthood?

I witnessed her put her family above all else
Sundays were ours to be with each other
evenings spent laughing at mediocre movies
sinner dinners if she was too tired to cook
a constant effort to conserve our consistency
if she could

And she always remained faithful
a bright light within the church
the perseverance to instill in us
the agency of our own faith
a stubbornness to denounce
the jaded views of all others
to provide us with the confidence that
God puts family above all else
a simple belief that maybe God just understood

I AM WHO RAISED ME pt. 2

My favorite trips were when
my father took me out on the road
strapped to the back of a bike
I saw the world outside the Utah scope
learned not to base salvation on
Sunday sacrament attendance
but to thank the tattooed trucker
who offered me his coat
learned not to villainize a vice
to love those who thought life
on Earth would suffice
to see the world is bigger
and much more beautiful
when perception is permitted to grow

HAVE I EVER FELT THE SPIRIT?

If the holy spirit is peace within the soul
I heard it when my grandfather would sing
I felt it in the goosebumps prickling my skin from beneath
I saw it in the embrace of my family
grateful for a day where we could just be
laughter filling the garden
a moment preserved just to breathe
a moment between it and me

THE COMMUNITY

A hundred threads
braided and banded and tied at the ends
a quilt to surround and shelter from the storm
a net to catch those who believe themselves forlorn
as strength is found in numbers
so is comfort when wrapped in its warmth

TESTIMONY

I liked to bear my testimony
a testament of my soul
an aching desire to testify
the truth in those teachings
I always said, "I know"
never, "I believe"
I followed every prompting
I prayed
I studied

I was never given any reason to doubt

CALLED TO SERVE

The soul is lost and weary
a divine purpose ripped from its grasp
the anchor is cast
you will not move forward
with this fleet

Provided a ship that only sinks
expected to brave the waves
the dry shore awaits
but there is no safe passage back
no welcoming cry for defeat

For it is better never to have gone
than to come home early
flaws found in surely
a dishonorable discharge
desire does not wait for the weak

Where there is no valor found
the saint who did not deliver
must be branded a sinner
but how does one sail
if blind in the darkness at sea?

MISSION

My greatest failure is no fault of my own
In the hour of need I was quietly dismissed
Sister, as a woman, you never needed to serve
Surrender your desire to go
In time you'll be fine
Once you become a mother and a wife
No need to mourn a position you could never fulfill

I'M FINE

I was desperate to be needed
screaming through the smile
my teeth smothering the sound of
inadequacy and doubt
I was unwanted

Unaware were friends who only heard the sounds
I chose to surrender
if only I had opened my mouth

sarah jane pyper

SOMETIMES BLESSINGS DON'T COME TRUE

A prophecy passed through a patriarch
placed hands on my head
pledged for me to be
a provider to preach to people
a prayer to prevail

Was the predetermined plan paused
or was I promised to fail?

GUILTLESS

I apologized for sins I never committed
trained to own blame to protect the self-
proclaimed guiltless
I held knives in my hands
blood dripping to witness
a one-sided battle
unforgiving
and
bliss-less

I LOVE TO SEE THE TEMPLE

As a child I sang the song
watched those around me
praise my faith
praise my reliability to maintain my standards
standards placed upon my head
and fed through my ear

I shouldn't be uncomfortable here

As a teenager I worked to grow my worth
validated my effort through self-effacing speeches
thwarted the twists and turns of temptation
found faith through the fear

I shouldn't be uncomfortable here

As an adult I reached the temple
high expectations gripping my stomach
bestowed upon me a sacred privilege
a proof of my worthiness
a proof of the sacrifice I'd given through the years

I shouldn't be uncomfortable here

Now I am a saint
a spirit who has found its way home
I witness holy worship
privy to the patriarch's preaches
while justifications from my matriarch
are fed through my ear

I am uncomfortable here

HAPPY VALLEY

When did it change?

Instead of everyone
going to church to
try to be their best
it's a show of everyone
trying to prove
they are the best

A gloss adorned every Sunday

MIXED FAITH

Rumors spread
like a wildfire to a wasteland
what should it matter
his faith or lack of
if his faith lies in us
not a deity from above
but when asked if
my decision was definite
when asked if
it would have been better to leave
how was I not to believe
when he was with me
I could so soundly sleep
tell me
how is that not peace
how is that not a sacred relief
to love and be loved
regardless of belief

FATE

For all those who question
belief before betrothal
know faith was what
led me to him
and God played chaperone

SOULMATE

You looked at me like a sailor would
a lighthouse guiding him to shore
a brightness reflected off your iris
a confidence in who you decided
was yours
and I knew you were sure

I looked at you like a sailor would
the sea she has yet to explore
excitement bursting from my eyelids
a decision to make you
my core
and you knew I was sure

HEAVEN

I love everything about who
you are
my heaven
but I'd give up
heaven
if I knew I'd have to fall
to keep
you

CANYON

If from the ground I stared up at the leaves
would I become the wind
to freeze my cheeks
I need to breathe
will you drive me up the canyon?
help me leave?
so I can breathe
so I can breathe
drive me up the canyon
I need the peace
I need the trees
I need to breathe
drive me up the canyon
please

PEACE ON SUNDAYS

I somehow found solace among the mountains
there was always truth found in
"peace on Sundays" if I found myself there
a chance to relax an anxious mind
to breathe through the fluttering heartbeats that
confined my lungs and forced them to constrict
where I could avoid panic
where I could avoid expectation
and simply be
just be

DURING

DECEPTION

How can it be
the place I once relied on to feel peace
now brings the most turmoil
and rattles my soul?

GOOD ENOUGH

I sit in my room and wait for the tears
Sunday always seems to bring
I've spent my whole life focusing on what's to come—
what wrong could I possibly be doing?
I promised my name
a willing exchange
for a life after death I believed
a once vivid dreamer
turned internal screamer
an impending doom I've conceived

STRAY

I have spent my life so focused on after I die
I will never be good enough . . . will I?

FAITH VERSUS FEAR

Am I continuing
led by what
above resides?
or am I continuing
paranoid to stop
what terror
awaits below?

Have I been pursuing
the light
or trying to outrun
the shadow?

FAITH CRISIS

Is faith the absence of fear
or are we so consumed by uncertainty
we never think to stray?

GUT INSTINCT

My unease is ravenous—
consuming me from inside out—
how am I to adorn armor
to defend against
my own doubt?

PUT IT ON THE SHELF FOR LATER

I was told to doubt my doubts
to leave whatever questions I have on the shelf
but I am being buried underneath the weight
and if I don't address them now
I'll be crushed

WHAT IS THE TRUTH?

I know that I'm allowed to question
when I have doubts
the expectation being that it would always
lead me to the truth
but the more I research
the more I want to step away
and that terrifies me

STRAY

It is acceptable to question
unless I come to the wrong conclusion

.

SELFLESS

I gave them all the air from my lungs
and now I forget how to breathe

DOUBT

How am I supposed to have faith in a plan
that never goes according to plan?

INDECISION

I am surrounded by others' opinions
constantly calculating consequences
forfeiting my own decisions
if I tell her, I'm condemned
if I tell him, I'm commended
I'm a rope within a tug-of-war
unaware of where the end is

PERMISSION

I want to run
but I haven't given myself permission
excuses branded as intuition
but now I'm centered between all decisions
and can't decide where to go

P R A Y E R

Please tell me my soul isn't
Ruined if I continue to
Allow myself to question my
Youthful innocence and undoubting mind. I'm
Eager to
Recognize the truth

QUESTIONING

I remember the moment I allowed myself
to go there
to peek underneath the door and
slowly grasp the handle
twisting until it opened
anxiety rushing over me like
a wave rushing the shore

To stand in the doorway and see
nothing but emptiness
emptiness I have yet to explore
to take a step into the darkness
and finally feel
relief

MODESTY

I have the responsibility of teaching
boys how to behave
by covering my own body
their souls will be saved
why is it the responsibility of women
to watch over men's minds?
it's an insult to both of us—
preaching that men can't control themselves
and women must hide

EQUALITY

How are we expected to be the same
when we can't speak our Heavenly Mother's name?

How are we to believe we are represented
when I look to the podium and see only men stand?

MATRIARCH

I was raised by women who fight back
a matriarch of warriors with
tiger teeth and lion hearts
patient predators who sacrificed everything for those
they fought to protect
a loving pride
who filled me with pride to speak the words
I am woman
who taught me never to justify
who taught me how to say no

STRAY

So why do I question
why I now question
what I used to believe?

I am woman

I will fight back

I will not justify

I will say no

BLACK AND WHITE THINKING

They must have the unique ability
to pick and choose
who to believe and what to refuse
I've been unable to separate—
my fatal flaw—
what is of man
versus
what comes from God

MOUTHPIECE OF GOD

How am I expected to discern man from God?
when leaders have been consistently proven wrong
all works of apostles are righteous and true
until thirty years on when time morphs our view
if God is always good but man makes mistakes
when can their words be deemed out of place?

HOW COULD LOVE BE A TRIAL

Our purpose on Earth
to love
to be loved
to accept we are created
shaped by the stars
and guided toward
celestial peace

To discover our soulmate
our greatest gifts
our family
to love for all eternity
unconditionally

But to another being
love is different
equally beautiful
powerful
shaped by the stars
as any other love
but
conditional

For them
to love is to sin
to love is to grieve
to obey they must break another belief
their purpose
to lie to themselves
and all others
an ultimatum for eternity

STRAY

To second guess their heart
undermine their feelings
question their core values
question their own being

But is this their trial
their burden to carry
to watch everyone around them love
and think they'll never be worthy

Well
I refuse to believe
an all-knowing
all-loving
God with a plan
would ever think it
a purposeful guide
to compose his child's
earthly trial
love itself

sarah jane pyper

IF GOD IS ALL-KNOWING

If God is all-knowing
why does the church constantly change its mind?
digging in its heels
until society deems it unethical and out of line
does God only care
about equality and lives
when the number of members continues to decline?

TRUST

It's not your fault I don't trust you
you're trudging past bodies who
plastered the bricks and constructed the wall
you now have to scale
and if you fall
it's as if you never began the journey
in the first place

DARK NIGHT FOR THE SOUL

Doubt erodes my stomach
guilt rips my heart
grief clouds my vision
and tears me apart
I try to preserve my feelings
like a dragon would hoard
it was never my intention to fail
but I'll fall on the sword
this will destroy me
my desire for truth
I don't want to leave
but I think I might have to

NIGHT OWL

I stay awake at night
it's much easier to face the demons
under my bed
than the ones
I create in my mind

FACADE

I am consumed by envy—
ignorance is not always bliss
but I look over and see
sterling smiles sustaining
a faith stronghold

My fortress
    is crumbling in solitude

But what I would give to feel
that kind of comfort again

I DON'T RELATE TO YOU ANYMORE

I am surrounded
but feel so alone
a silent outcast around them
Peter Pan barred from the window

PARANOID

I am filled with a guilt
not my own
the voice of a mother pleading
brothers screaming
violent red emotion
disguised as concern and
misleading
I'm only trying to define my own home
what if I'm wrong?
what if I'm wrong?
my mind weeps
this is how I will end up alone

DRIVE

I drive to sort my feelings through
sight of the headlights and the motion
force my mind
to focus on the moving objects ahead
on the moving forces in my head

GOOD PERSON

Am I a good person?
I volunteer my time at a foundation that
protects women from violence
Am I a good person?
I tried wine for the first time and liked it
Am I a good person?
I adopted my cat from a local animal shelter
Am I a good person?
I stopped going to church
Am I a good person?
I still talk to my mother every day
Am I a good person?
I feel happier away from religion
Am I a good person?
I've always been a listening ear to those in need
Am I a good person?
I don't know if I believe in God anymore
Am I a good person?
Am I a good person?

Hello?

INSECURITY

I'm waiting for the moment
your patience grows so thin
one exhale of my breath
will cause us to t
                e
                  a
                r

PASSION

I can feel my skin splitting—
peeking through the cracks flicker
flame extensions of my heart

Is this passion engulfing my spirit
or anger ripping me apart?

ENDLESS CYCLE

I allow myself to take a step back—
I feel relieved
but overwhelmed with guilt and grief
I was told I couldn't be this happy

So why am I so happy?

CONFESSION

My hands shake as I dial
I've been practicing my monologue—
how do I present this to you?
every worst-case scenario
every possible wrong turn
this conversation could take
an endless loop in my head
in sync with the ringing
tones as I anxiously await "hello"
and all I want to know at the end of this is

Will you still love me?

DISAPPOINTMENT

I'd spend a lifetime disappointing myself
to avoid disappointing you

GRIEF AND RELIEF

I was raised to believe I
was one of the lucky ones
the few blessed enough
to enjoy eternal elation
before eternity
condemned to confine my conscious mind
to the total belief
I will never be happier on the outside
is that why this guilt resides?
guilt bred and built on the foundation
my happiness
has to be a lie
so I cry
  and I cry
   and I cry
until I'm drowning underwater
begging God to keep my head under
just a little longer
devastated to determine my deterrence
to recognize my relief
if only I allowed myself to
come up for air and breathe

STRAY

Granting power to my own perception
void of sin but is this still a confession
that I feel more like myself
getting pierced in a tattoo parlor
than I ever did
praying in a pew
maybe it's time

                to

              take

                a

              step

              back

            farther

            to gain a different point of view

PROTECTED

I was raised in fire and fields of flowers
smoke impeding the vision of what lay
beyond the beautiful roses
that grew with me

But was I protected?
while I picked thorns from my feet each time I stepped
toward what I needed to find
the smoke-filled air invading my lungs
until I had no choice but to run from the flames

And maybe the fire wasn't there to protect
but to contain
maybe my family isn't perfect
maybe my mother makes mistakes

BETRAYAL

What I once mistook for wings
were chains wrenching my bones
back to the ground I so desperately
fought to jump from
if only I had turned around—
I might have preserved my back before being
dragged to my grave

sarah jane pyper

I FELL FOR IT

Will I be branded an angry woman?
desperate to scream out my shame—
to step from the ledge and curse at the ones
who promised I could float
if I only had faith, but
I am not angry
I am not ashamed
I am heartbroken
and I scream from the pain of my broken bones

P R A Y E R pt. 2

People used to tell me if I
Really meant it when I
Asked for your blessing
You would answer but now all I see are
Empty promises and forgotten
Remnants of my once strong belief

ROOTS

I was not cut down like the other trees
with the ability to grow back what was lost
my roots were wrenched up from the soil
nothing to remain but an empty void
a remnant of what once stood
a glorious and magnificent giant

BEGINNING

I am falling
wind tearing through ripped wings
faith lost in the divine
breath lost to realize
I can no longer fly

Will I cast a net
to catch my body as I crash?
a safety I earn as I yearn to detach

To find a new purpose
relearn to walk Earth is
my fall
a new season
a chance to find new belief in
something greater
than myself?

AFTER

THE INDIVIDUALIST

I made the hardest decision
and people claim I took the easy way out

Me, an individual desperate to be loved
who defied her loved ones

Me, an individual desperate for a community
who left her community

Me, an individual
who has never made an individual decision

I decided what was best for me
it broke me
and it rebuilt me

THE EASY WAY OUT

I handed over my weapon and
stepped into the circle
I admitted I was a fraud
I volunteered for the shot

Don't you think the easy way out
would have been
to never leave the firing squad
in the first place?

STRAY

They will use this word against me:
Stray

What does it truly mean to go astray?
to give up?
to fall behind?
because I didn't
I ran ahead until my lungs gave out
I jumped off the deep end and stayed there
till I drowned
I was let down
I never strayed
a strong believer once
now betrayed

AM I ALLOWED?

My spirit was ripped from my body
an extension of my soul I now find foreign
am I allowed to be angry?
my entire belief system redefined
a healing process requiring me to start from scratch
am I allowed to be angry?
deserted from my community
my identity erased
a stranger to my family they now find foreign
am I allowed to be angry?

ENOUGH

My worth was a mathematical equation
and I was not privy to the answer
when was enough?
when had I done enough?
donated enough of my money
donated enough of my time
enough of my spirit
enough of my mind

It is only when I scream
enough
I find my own worthiness
my self redefined

SELFISH

I am still untangling
the knotted concepts
in my mind

What is selfish?

And what is simply
taking care of myself?

A LOOK INWARD

I've changed for good but not for the better
I'm still trying to find myself
I haven't yet met her

ENNEAGRAM

I found my worth in the lives of those around me
desperate for dependent relationships
constantly seeking validation and praise
my mouth watering for the words
I need you

As I grew
fleeting relationships drifted away
but my mindset never shifted
no one needs me now
but I still seek validation and praise
my perfectionism holding me hostage
be important to someone or be nothing
be perfect or be nothing

So I throw myself into work
and pray it will be enough achievement
to put my soul's cravings at ease

A T H E I S T

Always a negative connotation
To assume because one does not
Have faith in a deity they must be
Empty of morality, but those
I've encountered have far more
Strength in character than
Those who are only righteous because they are told to be

sarah jane pyper

FIT IN

I am one of many
a desperate soul born into a box
told to fold to fit in

I don't bend that way

STILL

I still spend my days
trying to convince myself I'm not a burden
I'm twenty-five
still longing for a friend
who calls me first

PRIZE

I am still trying to be good
        not to avoid a consequence
        not to obtain a death prize

Simply to be good

STRAY

I recognize this may be my only opportunity at life

BEHIND CLOSED DOORS

I know of the whispers behind closed doors
I was once in the room
sharing spite masked as concern
the windows are barred
the door is locked
but you are always welcome
if only to mock

UNCONDITIONAL

I used to think I knew unconditional love
until I took a step back
from what I used to believe
and you took a step back
from me

ARE YOU STILL PROUD OF ME?

Are you still proud of me?
you smile at my face but
pray in earnest when I leave
do you pray for me to change?
do you wish I never changed?

PERCEPTION

I haven't changed
your perception of me has

IRON ROD

I became lost clinging to the iron rod
I stood in the fog and froze
desperate to find the reassurance that lay in "obey"

Others proceed forward
their grip maintaining their motivation
to continue along the path

My knuckles are white

And the only way for me to progress
is to let go

YOU GRIEVE

It breaks me to know you are not angry
you are not upset
you are genuinely concerned

My happiness causes you pain
causes you anxiety

As if my salvation depended on what you did
wrong, but you did nothing wrong
and neither did I

I guess that's what breaks my heart the most—
I'm at my most content and most relieved

And all it's done is cause you to grieve

sarah jane pyper

SPEAK UP

I dare not
no need to upset my family
but I am lucky
they will not judge me

But what of the others
who weep through closed teeth?
do I dare
speak?

OSTRACIZED OUT OF LOVE

We feel your worry—
you will try to bring it up in a casual way
not asking us to come back
only sharing what you learned today
but when we don't want to stay
you'll believe it's the weight of our shame

We don't want to argue
we don't want to destroy your faith
we don't want anyone to experience this pain
to understand why we feel this way
to accept that maybe we were betrayed

We'll never share what we have to say
we'll accept that we'll never agree
we'll be selfless holding back our pain for your beliefs
we'll know that you will mourn
our souls that won't be saved
we'll grieve in silence knowing
you hold the weight of that blame

STEEL

I was molten, melted by the flames
molded into shape
by iron hands and stubborn gloves
refused each opportunity to explicate myself
spirit envisioned through the perspective of another
only perception to convince me
the warmth I used to seek
now burned

So I recoiled from the blaze
became my own weapon
a sharp wit to wield my mind
in its purest form
to witness my own worth reborn

STRAY

They may now think me cold
but I have never felt
more conviction
away from the flame
that shaped me

GHOST

I want to be transparent
though I know all you'll see is
a ghost
a grief born from belief once inherent
a spirit ripped out of
the host

But it's you who will mourn
the lonely ship bright with fire
an arrow through the chest
I'll adorn
the pain reaped from those who desire
those who view my soul
as expired

MOSAIC

I take a hammer to my core
smashing my soul and ripping out values
I once considered essential
my mind was built on what others told me to be
a voice in the back of my head that
never belonged to me
now I am picking up the pieces
creating a new mosaic
who I was
and who I want to become

ORDINARY

I feel completely ordinary—
I don't know whether to be elated
or terrified
I'm no longer running after perfection
chasing an afterlife

Ordinary
a fresh start
a good place to try

VALIDATION

Now that I'm not seeking validation from above
or from those around me
who have never done enough
who am I?
what am I to do to find success?

                  I'm learning how to define happiness

WITHOUT

I have spent so much time looking up for guidance
blindly being led through what
I assumed were treacherous landscapes
but when self-governed and given
the ability to stare straight ahead
I see only open plains and endless possibilities

BATS AND BIRDS

I was told I needed feathers to fly
so I spread out my wings and
glued each one to my sides
each day I'd prepare and leap toward the view
and each day I'd fall while the other birds flew

It wasn't until I let myself recognize
the feathers I bore were a weight in disguise
while they helped to lift others
they burdened my wings
I realized I'm different—
I screech while the other birds sing

So when asked why I strayed away
why I no longer pursue the light
I show off my wings, smile, and say
I'm much more myself at night

NO STRINGS ATTACHED

I let go of my beliefs and open my arms
no justifications can tie my hands and
prevent me from throwing out my support
no lingering
but
to follow the words
I accept you
I am more empathetic
I am more caring
and I have the ability to love
without questioning

NO NEED TO MOURN THE HAPPY

Do not mourn those with genuine smiles
and eyes bright with relief
we have not lost ourselves on this journey
we lost your eternity
but discovered what it means
to be happy

DANDELION

It is not someone else's responsibility
to validate my existence
they will avoid the cracks that I continue
to exist in
it is up to me to grow
to flourish in self-esteem
prove my worth
is that of a flower
not a weed

LEADER

The day she finds confidence in herself the earth will fall
beneath her
the grounded weight once on her back
now a relic
not a follower, a leader

HAND TO HOLD

I had to walk this path alone
I had to trudge through the shadows
with each step
unraveling the ropes of grief from my feet
untying the blindfold that constricted my view
allowing myself to discover my own light

What is spirituality without guidance?
who am I without guidance?

No one could have answered this for me

But you played patient partner
comforter to my soul
you took each step in pace with mine
no matter how slow the journey

I had to walk this path alone
but thanks to you
I had a hand to hold

THANK YOU

You allowed me to question
without ever questioning me

You allowed me to doubt
without ever doubting me

That meant everything

RECONCILE

I hear the waves crashing against the rocks
outside the window where we've spent all night
delving into ourselves, our innermost beliefs
until 3 am
when I sent myself to bed
we connected for hours on end
I had the opportunity
to speak with you on a level
we never dared tread before
because now I get it
you can speak and be seen
because now I get it
and I can learn
and I can forgive
and I can be grateful that I've gone through this
because it's given me
you

REGRET

I'd like to think it would have been better
you would have been honest
secure in our relationship
shared feelings through letters
maybe our bond would not have been
as strained as it became

But mistakes were made

I'd like to think that it had nothing to do with belief
that I was not consumed by consequence
afraid for your salvation
never showing you my grief
that maybe my concerns
wrapped forgiveness in a cage

There are lessons that can only be learned with age

I'd like to think I walked away with no regret
that I knew our past was absolved
moved through our pain
and learned to forget
that maybe I've forgiven myself for putting
faith before a father

Now that we are walking the bridge over water

I HAVE FAITH

Faith:
A complete trust or confidence
in someone or something

I have faith
faith in my family
faith in my friends
faith in my love
faith in myself

I may have lost faith in heaven
but I gained it somewhere else

ACCEPTANCE

I show up to the gathering
eyes light at the faces of so many
I haven't visited in months
it brings me joy
to recognize how lucky I am
to be welcomed in tight embrace
and greetings of laughter
to know that I am still loved
to accept that things haven't changed
apart from me
and I can walk into a room
and know for a fact
my family will love me
exactly the way I am

GRATEFUL FOR MY PAST

A butterfly
looks back at their cocoon
not with malice but
with gratitude
without that shelter
without that marinating time
it would never have gained
the ability
to fly

GOD IS

God is the relief knowing my parents both got
the love they deserve
God is the release that comes when
I forgive the lessons learned
God is the capability to believe those
who exemplified their change
God is the laughter that fills my lungs
when I look back at my pain
God is the tranquility I feel now
I'm content within myself
God is the smile of my mother
      the bear hugs from my brothers
          the trust between my lover
all the peace I've ever felt

THIS IS YOUR JOURNEY

You walk alone on your path
overcoming your individual woes and wrath
wary of the whispering woods you avert
but grateful for the trees once past
the burden of a desert

Scars mark your body
the bruises and cuts from the weeds
your tumbles creating canvases of
scrapes on your knees

But this is your journey

And those who walk their path
may use different tools
sage advice may only be that of a fool's

But this is your journey

And there is no one right way for all
no destined quest to befall
there is only that which is right for you
what expedition peace will guide you to do

This is your journey

TRAIN

I can be grateful for my past
without entwining it to my future
pack my morals and values
like heirlooms in a suitcase
leave with a parting gesture
as I catch the last train toward
what is to come

As forgive and forget are twin flames
so should be reflect and evolve
reminiscent of a revival
a sequel standing on her own
a solo track played
on top the sound of the tracks
on this new route
I'm viewing from the cabin window

About the Author

sarah jane pyper was raised in the valley surrounded by mountains and ski slopes and now resides in the land of cacti and rattlesnakes. She has spent years writing poetry and prose for her personal journaling, but this is her first published work. She's often dreamed of sharing her words with the world in hopes that she could deliver a story to relate to and warm the hearts of others. When she's not writing, you can find her relaxing at home with her husband, Nathan, and their little zoo of two cats and three snakes.

Connect with her on social media:

Instagram: @pyperpoetry
TikTok: @sarahjanepyperpoetry
Website: www.sarahjanepyper.com

www.ingramcontent.com/pod-product-compliance
Lightning Source LLC
Chambersburg PA
CBHW070720130626
46553CB00005B/2082